Praise for
THE 637 BEST THINGS ANYBODY EVER SAID

"It is a good thing for an educated man
to read books of quotations."
Winston Churchill

"The intelligent man finds almost
everything ridiculous."
Goethe

"This book fills a much-needed gap."
Moses Hadas

"There is nothing so absurd
but some philospher has said it."
Cicero

"Crude, immoral, vulgar, and senseless."
Tolstoy

The

637

Best things anybody ever said

The whole chosen and arranged by

ROBERT BYRNE

And presented with a few of the
best things Robert Byrne ever said

FAWCETT CREST • NEW YORK

CONTENTS

INTRODUCTION

Many of the best things ever said were, in fact, written. Aside from that, the title of this book is accurate.

The quotations are arranged with readers rather than the alphabet in mind. By readers I mean people who normally start at the front of a book and digest the pages consecutively; I don't mean those who intend to turn to a given subject heading in hopes of finding a smart remark. There are no subject headings.

The arrangement is intended to have a cumulative effect, with an occasional interactive juxtaposition. This is especially true in Part One, where the entries are grouped under loosely defined themes. In Part Two the sequence is governed by subjective criteria that even I don't fully understand.

Most collections of quotations strive for such things as comprehensiveness, balance, and fairness. Not this one.

No attempt is made to cite every major author, authority, and humorist.

No attempt is made to include a quote from every topic or from every epoch.

While it is undeniably interesting and perhaps even important to discover that Martin Luther (1483–1546) was the first to point out that it depends on whose ox is gored, no quotes were included merely to teach history or establish priorities.

The book is simply a compilation of the best things anybody ever said. The entries are characterized by their insight, surprise, wit, pith, or punch. Because surprise was one of the elements I sought, some great remarks were left out on the grounds of excessive familiarity. No sense giving you a tour of your own living room. If you do spot some old friends here, I can only hope that you will be glad to see them again.

Some quotations take on added point when their age is known. For that reason and as a sop to scholars I have included birth and death dates for historical figures. Where no dates are given, it can be assumed that the person is either still alive or only lately dead.

Some may wonder why there are 637 quotations instead of, say, 631 or 643. The reason is that I didn't want any padding and I didn't want to leave any good ones out. I didn't know that the best things anybody ever said amounted to 637 until after I had sifted through the world's literature, oral traditions, and wisecracks.

But who, after all, can say what is "best"? I can. So can you. What follows are my choices. Now it may be that you have said, heard, written, or read something that merits inclusion in a cream-of-the-crop collection like this but which is missing because for one reason or another you simply have never called it to my attention. Whose fault is that? I'm as close as your mailbox.

Robert Byrne
% Atheneum Publishers
597 Fifth Avenue
New York, New York 10017

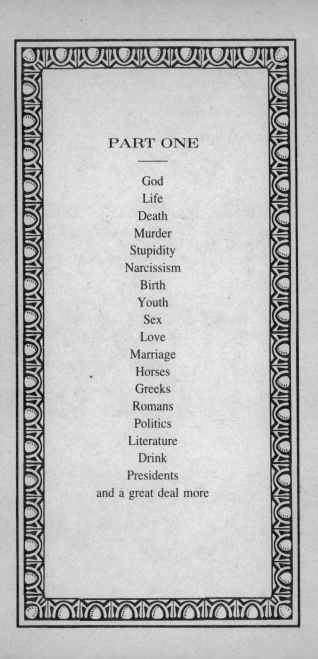

PART ONE

God
Life
Death
Murder
Stupidity
Narcissism
Birth
Youth
Sex
Love
Marriage
Horses
Greeks
Romans
Politics
Literature
Drink
Presidents
and a great deal more

1

Why don't you get a haircut? You look like a chrysanthemum. *P. G. Wodehouse (1911–1975)*

2

How can I believe in God when just last week I got my tongue caught in the roller of an electric typewriter? *Woody Allen*

3

If I had been present at creation, I would have given some useful hints. *Alfonso the Wise (1221–1284)*

4

The gods play games with men as balls.
Titus Maccius Platus (254?–184 B.C.)

5

He was a wise man who invented God.
Plato (427?–348? B.C.)

6

Plato is a bore. *Nietzsche (1844–1900)*

7

It is the final proof of God's omnipotence that he need not exist in order to save us. *Peter De Vries*

8

Man is a god in ruins. *Ralph Waldo Emerson (1803–1882)*

9

God has always been hard on the poor.
Jean Paul Marat (1743–1793)

Man is certainly stark mad. He cannot make a worm, and yet
he will be making gods by dozens.   *Montaigne (1553–1592)*

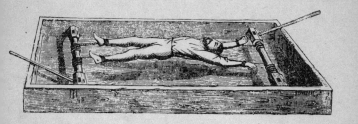

The good Lord never gives you more than you can handle.
Unless you die of something.   *Guindon cartoon caption*

If I had been the Virgin Mary, I would have said "No."
                    Margaret "Stevie" Smith (1902–1971)

Few people can be happy unless they hate some other person,
nation, or creed.   *Bertrand Russell (1872–1970)*

Religions change; beer and wine remain.
                    Hervey Allen (1889–1949)

The chicken probably came before the egg because it is hard to imagine God wanting to sit on an egg. *Unknown*

In England there are sixty different religions and only one sauce. *Francesco Caracciolo (1752–1799)*

Living with a saint is more grueling than being one.

Robert Neville

He was of the faith chiefly in the sense that the church he currently did not attend was Catholic. *Kingsley Amis*

Everybody should believe in something; I believe I'll have another drink. *Unknown*

Under certain circumstances, profanity provides a relief denied even to prayer. *Mark Twain (1835–1910)*

The trouble with born-again Christians is that they are an even bigger pain the second time around. *Herb Caen*

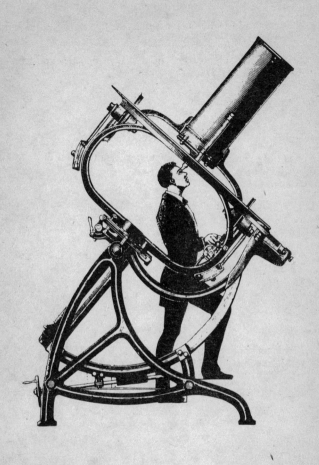

22

I'm astounded by people who want to "know" the universe when it's hard enough to find your way around China-town. *Woody Allen*

It is better to know some of the questions than all of the answers.   *James Thurber (1894–1961)*

24

It is only possible to live happily ever after on a day to day basis.   *Margaret Bonnano*

25

I have a new philosophy. I'm only going to dread one day at a time.   *Charles Schulz*

26

I have a simple philosophy. Fill what's empty. Empty what's full. Scratch where it itches.

Alice Roosevelt Longworth (1884–1980)

27

I know the answer! The answer lies within the heart of all mankind! The answer is twelve? I think I'm in the wrong building.   *Charles Schulz*

Life is like an overlong drama through which we sit being nagged by the vague memories of having read the reviews.   *John Updike*

29

There is more to life than increasing its speed.
Mahatma Gandhi (1869–1948)

30

Life is like playing a violin in public and learning the instrument as one goes on.   *Samuel Butler (1835–1902)*

31

Life is what happens while you are making other plans.
John Lennon (1940–1980)

Life is a God-damned, stinking, treacherous game and nine hundred and ninety-nine men out of a thousand are bastards.

Theodore Dreiser (1871–1945)
quoting an unnamed newspaper editor

❦

There is no cure for birth and death save to enjoy the interval. *George Santayana (1863–1952)*

Why is it that we rejoice at a birth and grieve at a funeral? It is because we are not the person involved.

Mark Twain (1835–1910)

The cost of living is going up and the chance of living is going down. *Flip Wilson*

Is life worth living? That depends on the liver. *Unknown*

Dying is one of the few things that can be done as easily lying down. *Woody Allen*

38

I'm not afraid to die. I just don't want to be there when it happens. *Woody Allen*

39

Perhaps there is no life after death...there's just Los Angeles. *Rich Anderson*

40

Death is nature's way of saying "Howdy." *Unknown*

41

The best way to get praise is to die. *Italian proverb*

42

There is no such thing as inner peace. There is only nervousness and death. *Fran Liebowitz*

43

In the long run we are all dead.
John Maynard Keynes (1883–1946)

44

The patient is not likely to recover who makes the doctor his heir. *Thomas Fuller (1608–1661)*

45

After I'm dead I'd rather have people ask why I have no monument than why I have one.   *Cato the Elder (234 – 149* B.C.*)*

46

For three days after death hair and fingernails continue to grow but phone calls taper off.   *Johnny Carson*

47

I wonder if anybody ever reached the age of thirty-five in New England without wanting to kill himself.
Barrett Wendell (1855 – 1921)

48

I have had just about all I can take of myself.
*S. N. Behrman (1893 – 1973) on reaching
the age of 75*

49

When you don't have any money, the problem is food. When you have money, it's sex. When you have both, it's health. If everything is simply jake, then you're frightened of death.
J. P. Donleavy

50

Most people would sooner die than think; in fact, they do so.   *Bertrand Russell (1872 – 1970)*

51

Early one June morning in 1872 I murdered my father—an act which made a deep impression on me at the time.
Ambrose Bierce (1842–1914)

52

One murder makes a villain, millions a hero.
Beilby Porteus (1731–1808)

53

If once a man indulges himself in murder, very soon he comes to think little of robbing; and from robbing he next comes to drinking and Sabbath-breaking, and from that to incivility and procrastination.   *Thomas De Quincey (1785–1859)*

54

A murderer is one who is presumed to be innocent until proven insane.   *Unknown*

55

Either this man is dead or my watch has stopped.
Groucho Marx (1890–1977)

56

There is no money in poetry, but then there is no poetry in money, either.   *Robert Graves*

57

This poem will never reach its destination.

Voltaire (1694–1778) on Rousseau's
Ode to Posterity

58

I hope that one or two immortal lyrics will come out of all this tumbling around.

Poet Louise Bogan (1898–1970) on her love
affair with poet Theodore Roethke

59

I write poetry not for publication but merely to kill time. Airplanes are a good place to write poetry and then firmly throw it away. My collected works are mostly on the vomit bags of Pan American and TWA. *Charles McCabe*

60

The writing of more than 75 poems in any fiscal year should be punishable by a fine of $500. *Ed Sanders*

61

Show me a poet and I'll show you a shit.

A. J. Liebling (1904–1963))

62

The human mind treats a new idea the way the body treats a strange protein; it rejects it.   *Biologist P. B. Medawar*

63

The intelligent man finds almost everything ridiculous, the sensible man hardly anything.   *Goethe (1749–1832)*

64

The difference between genius and stupidity is that genius has its limits.   *Unknown*

65

The only reason some people get lost in thought is because it's unfamiliar territory.   *Paul Fix*

66

Only the mediocre are always at their best.
Jean Giraudoux (1882–1944)

67

I'm going to speak my mind because I have nothing to lose.   *S. I. Hayakawa*

68

I live in the crowd of jollity, not so much to enjoy company as to shun myself.   *Samuel Johnson (1709–1784)*

69

For every ten jokes, thou hast got an hundred enemies.   *Laurence Sterne (1713–1768)*

70

Wit is educated insolence.   *Aristotle (384–322 B.C.)*

71

Seriousness is the only refuge of the shallow.
                              Oscar Wilde (1854–1900)

72

He who laughs, lasts.   *Mary Pettibone Poole (c. 1938)*

73

Man: An animal [whose] . . . chief occupation is extermination of other animals and his own species, which, however, multiplies with such insistent rapidity as to infest the whole habitable earth and Canada.   *Ambrose Bierce (1842–1914)*

Woman: An animal . . . having a rudimentary susceptibility to domestication . . . The species is the most widely distributed of all beasts of prey. . . . The woman is omnivorous and can be taught not to talk.   *Ambrose Bierce (1842–1914)*

Cabbage: A . . . vegetable about as large and wise as a man's head.   *Ambrose Bierce (1842–1914)*

Memorial Service: Farewell party for someone who has already left.   *RB*

Eunuch: A man who has had his works cut out for him.   *RB*

I hate definitions.   *Benjamin Disraeli (1804–1881)*

The affair between Margot Asquith and Margot Asquith will live as one of the prettiest love stories in all literature.
*Dorothy Parker (1893–1967) in a review
of a book by Margot Asquith*

80

To love oneself is the beginning of a life-long romance.

Oscar Wilde (1854—1900)

81

Like all self-made men he worships his creator. *Unknown*

82

Egotist: A person . . . more interested in himself than in me.
Ambrose Bierce (1842–1914)

83

A narcissist is someone better looking than you are.
Gore Vidal

84

Don't be humble. You're not that great.
Golda Meir (1898–1978)

85

Stop crime at its source! Support Planned Parenthood. *RB*

86

When turkeys mate they think of swans. *Johnny Carson*

87

Except during the nine months before he draws his first breath,
no man manages his affairs as well as a tree does.
George Bernard Shaw (1856–1950)

It is now quite lawful for a Catholic woman to avoid pregnancy by a resort to mathematics, though she is still forbidden to resort to physics or chemistry.

H. L. Mencken (1880–1956)

89

Somewhere on this globe, every ten seconds, there is a woman giving birth to a child. She must be found and stopped.
Sam Levenson (1911–1980)

90

To enter life by way of the vagina is as good a way as any.   *Henry Miller (1891–1980)*

91

I have an intense desire to return to the womb. Anybody's.   *Woody Allen*

92

To my embarrassment I was born in bed with a lady.
Wilson Mizner (1876–1933)

93

My obstetrician was so dumb that when I gave birth he forgot to cut the cord. For a year that kid followed me *everywhere*. It was like having a dog on a leash.   *Joan Rivers*

94

I knew I was an unwanted baby when I saw that my bath toys were a toaster and a radio.   *Joan Rivers*

95

A child is a curly, dimpled lunatic.
Ralph Waldo Emerson (1803–1882)

96

All children are essentially criminal.

Denis Diderot (1713–1784)

97

A vegetarian is a person who won't eat anything that can have children.   *David Brenner*

98

When I was a child what I wanted to be when I grew up was an invalid.   *Quentin Crisp*

99

Children of the poor should work for some part of the day when they reach the age of three.

John Locke (1632–1704) in 1697

100

Of all the animals, the boy is the most unmanageable.

Plato (427?–348? B.C.)

Plato is a bore.   *Nietzsche (1844–1900)*

101

Children are guilty of unpardonable rudeness when they spit in the face of a companion; neither are they excusable who spit from windows or on walls or furniture.

St. John Baptist de La Salle (c. 1695)

102

Thank God kids never mean well.   *Lily Tomlin*

103

Mothers are fonder than fathers of their children because they are more certain they are their own.

Aristotle (384–322 B.C.)

104

There's nothing wrong with teenagers that reasoning with them won't aggravate.   *Unknown*

105

Young people are more hopeful at a certain age than adults, but I suspect that's glandular. As for children, I keep as far from them as possible. I don't like the sight of them. The scale is all wrong. The heads tend to be too big for the bodies, and the hands and feet are a disaster. They keep falling into things. The nakedness of their bad character! We adults have learned how to disguise our terrible character, but children, well, they are like grotesque drawings of *us*. They should be neither seen nor heard, and no one must make another one.   *Gore Vidal*

106

I tell you I can feel them! They're all around us! Young people! Getting closer and closer!   *Hamilton cartoon caption*

107

The reason husband and wives do not understand each other
is because they belong to different sexes.

Dorothy Dix (1870–1951)

108

There was a time when we expected nothing of children but
obedience, as opposed to the present, when we expect everything of them but obedience.   *Anatole Broyard*

109

The reason grandparents and grandchildren get along so well
is that they have a common enemy.

Sam Levenson (1911–1980)

110

I never met a kid I liked.   *W. C. Fields (1880–1946)*

111

It is a good thing for an uneducated man to read books of
quotations.   *Winston Churchill (1874–1965)*

112

I hate quotations.   *Ralph Waldo Emerson (1803–1882)*

113

If men could get pregnant, abortion would be a sacrament. *Florynce Kennedy*

❧◉❧

114

Ever since the young men have owned motorcycles, incest has been dying out. *Max Frisch*

115

Familiarity breeds attempt.

Goodman Ace (1899–1982)

116

Sex drive: A physical craving that begins in adolescence and ends at marriage. *RB*

117

Sex is the most fun you can have without smiling.

Unknown

118

I would rather go to bed with Lillian Russell stark naked than Ulysses S. Grant in full military regalia.

Mark Twain (1835–1910)

119

Last time I tried to make love to my wife nothing was happening, so I said to her, "What's the matter, you can't think of anybody either?" *Rodney Dangerfield*

120

If it weren't for pickpockets I'd have no sex life at all.

Rodney Dangerfield

121

I've tried several varieties of sex. The conventional position makes me claustrophobic and the others give me a stiff neck or lockjaw. *Tallulah Bankhead (1903–1968)*

122

A woman occasionally is quite a serviceable substitute for masturbation. *Karl Kraus*

123

Sex is nobody's business except the three people involved. *Unknown*

124

What men desire is a virgin who is a whore.
Edward Dahlberg (1900–1977)

125

The orgasm has replaced the Cross as the focus of longing and the image of fulfillment. *Malcolm Muggeridge*

All this fuss about sleeping together. For physical pleasure I'd sooner go to my dentist any day.

Evelyn Waugh (1903–1966)

What a man enjoys about a woman's clothes are his fantasies of how she would look without them.   *Brendan Francis*

128

Women who miscalculate are called "mothers."

Abigail Van Buren

129

Nothing is so much to be shunned as sex relations.

St. Augustine (354–430)

130

I kissed my first girl and smoked my first cigarette on the same day. I haven't had time for tobacco since.

Arturo Toscanini (1867–1957)

131

The only really indecent people are the chaste.

J. K. Huysmans (1848–1907)

132

For the preservation of chastity, an empty and rumbling stomach and fevered lungs are indispensable.

St. Jerome (340?–420)

133

I hate women because they always know where things are. *James Thurber (1894–1961)*

134

Sex is the biggest nothing of all time. *Andy Warhol*

❧⊙H⊙❧

Love is the delightful interval between meeting a beautiful girl and discovering that she looks like a haddock.

John Barrymore (1882–1942)

Love is an ocean of emotions entirely surrounded by expenses. *Lord Dewar*

Love is a grave mental disease. *Plato (427?–348? B.C.)*

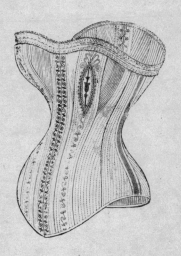

Whatever deceives seems to produce a magical enchantment. *Plato (427?–348? B.C.)*

Plato is a bore. *Nietzsche (1844–1900)*

139

The heaviest object in the world is the body of the woman you have ceased to love.

Marquis de Luc de Clapiers Vauvenargues
(1715–1747)

140

In expressing love we belong among the undeveloped countries. *Saul Bellow*

141

A man can be happy with any woman as long as he does not love her. *Oscar Wilde (1854–1900)*

142

Love will find a lay. *RB*

143

It takes a woman twenty years to make a man of her son, and another woman twenty minutes to make a fool of him.

Helen Rowland (1876–1950)

144

It is better to have loved and lost than never to have lost at all. *Samuel Butler (1835–1902)*

145

I sold my memoirs of my love life to Parker Brothers and they are going to make a game out of it. *Woody Allen*

146

The only solid and lasting peace between a man and his wife is doubtless a separation.   *Lord Chesterfield (1694–1773)*

147

Marriage: A master, a mistress and two slaves, making in all, two.   *Ambrose Bierce (1842–1914)*

148

Marriage is not a word but a sentence.   *Unknown*

149

Marriage is a great institution, but I'm not ready for an institution.   *Mae West (1893–1980)*

150

If I ever marry it will be on a sudden impulse, as a man shoots himself.   *H. L. Mencken (1880–1956)*

151

For the upper middle class, marriage is the only adventure left.   *Unknown*

152

We want playmates we can own.   *Jules Feiffer on marriage*

It was so cold I almost got married.   *Shelley Winters*

At American weddings, the quality of the food is inversely proportional to the social position of the bride and groom.   *Calvin Trillin*

I was married once. Now I just lease.

From the movie Buddy, Buddy (*1981*)

156

I married beneath me. All women do.
> Nancy, Lady Astor (1879–1964)

157

An archeologist is the best husband a woman can have; the older she gets, the more interested he is in her.
> Agatha Christie (1891–1976),
> who was married to one

158

I tended to place my wife under a pedestal.   *Woody Allen*

159

My mother-in-law broke up my marriage. One day my wife came home early from work and found us in bed together.   *Lenny Bruce (1926–1966)*

160

Divorce is the sacrament of adultery.   *French proverb*

161

What scares me about divorce is that my children might put me in a home for unwed mothers.   *Teressa Skelton*

162

Take my wife ... please! *Henny Youngman*

163

A CURSE

May your soul be forever tormented by fire and your bones be dug up by dogs and dragged through the streets of Minneapolis. *Garrison Keillor*

164

My work is done, why wait?

Suicide note left by Kodak founder
George Eastman (1854–1932)

165

All right, then, I'll say it: Dante makes me sick.

Last words of Spanish playwright
Lope de Vega on being assured on his
deathbed that the end was very near.

166

I don't feel good.   *Last words of Luther Burbank (1849–1926)*

167

Don't let it end like this. Tell them I said something.

Last words of Pancho Villa (1877?–1923)

168

It is better to be a coward for a minute than dead for the rest
of your life.   *Irish proverb*

169

The reverse side also has a reverse side.   *Japanese proverb*

170

Tell the truth and run.   *Yugloslavian proverb*

171

Do not insult the mother alligator until after you have crossed the river. *Haitian proverb*

172

Too clever is dumb. *German proverb*

173

The Irish ignore anything they can't drink or punch.

Old saying

174

If God lived on earth, people would break his windows.

Jewish proverb

175

It is nothing, they are only thrashing my husband.

Portuguese proverb

176

When the cat and mouse agree, the grocer is ruined.

Persian proverb

177

I do not say a proverb is amiss when aptly and reasonably applied, but to be forever discharging them, right or wrong, hit or miss, renders conversation insipid and vulgar.

Miguel Cervantes (1547–1616)

178

Wise men make proverbs but fools repeat them.

Samuel Palmer (c. 1710)

179

Nobody has ever bet enough on the winning horse.

Overheard at a track by Richard Sasuly

180

One of the worst things that can happen in life is to win a bet on a horse at an early age.   *Danny McGoorty (1901–1970)*

181

Nobody ever committed suicide who had a good two-year-old in the barn.   *Racetrack proverb*

182

It is morally wrong to allow suckers to keep their money.   *"Canada Bill" Jones*

183

All life is six to five against.   *Damon Runyon (1884–1946)*

184

Much as he is opposed to lawbreaking, he is not bigoted about it.   *Damon Runyon (1884–1946)*

185

You might as well fall flat on your face as lean over too far backward.   *James Thurber (1894–1961)*

186

Alexander III of Macedonia is known as Alexander the Great because he killed more people of more different kinds than any other man of his time.   *Will Cuppy (1884–1949)*

187

Aristotle was famous for knowing everything. He taught that the brain exists merely to cool the blood and is not involved in the process of thinking. This is true only of certain persons.
Will Cuppy (1884–1949)

188

All Gaul is divided into three parts: igneous, metamorphic, and sedimentary. *Geologist Wilson Hinckley (1928–1972)*

189

What a time! What a civilization! *Cicero (106–43 B.C.)*

190

Oh, this age! How tasteless and ill-bred it is!
Catullus (87?–54? B.C.)

191

How little you know about the age you live in if you think that honey is sweeter than cash in hand.
Ovid (43? B.C.–A.D. 18)

192

It is sometimes expedient to forget who we are.
Publilius Syrus (c. 42 B.C.)

193

There is no glory in outstripping donkeys.   *Martial (40–102)*

194

The school of hard knocks is an accelerated curriculum.
Menander (342?–292? B.C.)

195

There is nothing so absurd but some philosopher has said it.
Cicero (106–43 B.C.)

196

A man with his belly full of the classics is an enemy of the human race. *Henry Miller (1891–1980)*

197

Patriotism is the willingness to kill and be killed for trivial reasons. *Bertrand Russell (1872–1970)*

198

Democracy substitutes election by the incompetent many for appointment by the corrupt few.
George Bernard Shaw (1856–1950)

American has been discovered before, but it has always been hushed up.   *Oscar Wilde (1854–1900)*

The 100% American is 99% an idiot.
                    George Bernard Shaw (1856–1950)

A government which robs Peter to pay Paul can always depend on the support of Paul.   *George Bernard Shaw (1856–1950)*

And that's the world in a nutshell—an appropriate receptacle.   *Stan Dunn*

The remarkable thing about Shakespeare is that he really is very good, in spite of all the people who say he is very good.   *Robert Graves*

Crude, immoral, vulgar, and senseless.
                    Tolstoy (1882–1910) on Shakespeare

205

I know not, sir, whether Bacon wrote the works of Shakespeare, but if he did not it seems to me that he missed the opportunity of his life.   *James Barrie (1860–1937)*

206

If Shakespeare had been in pro basketball he never would have had time to write his soliloquies. He would always have been on a plane between Phoenix and Kansas City.

Paul Westhead, basketball coach

207

A team is a team is a team. Shakespeare said that many times.   *Dan Devine, football coach*

208

A piano is a piano is a piano.—Gertrude Steinway

Unknown

209

A manuscript, like a foetus, is never improved by showing it to somebody before it is completed.   *Unknown*

210

Every journalist has a novel in him, which is an excellent place for it.   *Russell Lynes*

211

Why authors write I do not know. As well ask why a hen lays an egg or a cow stands patiently while a farmer burglarizes her.   *H. L. Mencken (1880–1956)*

212

Why do writers write? Because it isn't there.

Thomas Berger

213

Never let a domestic quarrel ruin a day's writing. If you can't start the next day fresh, get rid of your wife.

*One of Mario Puzo's rules for writing
a best-selling novel*

214

Every novel should have a beginning, a muddle, and an end.   *Peter De Vries*

215

Boy meets girl; girl gets boy into pickle; boy gets pickle into girl.   *Jack Woodford (1894–1971) on plotting*

Writing is easy. All you do is stare at a blank sheet of paper until drops of blood form on your forehead.
Gene Fowler (1890–1960)

With a novelist, like a surgeon, you have to get a feeling that you've fallen into good hands—someone from whom you can accept the anesthetic with confidence. *Saul Bellow*

Sometimes when reading Goethe I have a paralyzing suspicion that he is trying to be funny. *Guy Davenport*

The novelist, afraid his ideas may be foolish, slyly puts them in the mouth of some other fool and reserves the right to disavow them. *Diane Johnson*

He can compress the most words into the smallest idea of any man I ever met. *Abraham Lincoln (1809–1865)*

If a writer has to rob his mother he will not hesitate; the *Ode On a Grecian Urn* is worth any number of old ladies.
William Faulkner (1897–1962)

222

In literature as in love, we are astonished at what is chosen by others. *André Maurois (1885–1967)*

223

It is a delicious thing to write, to be no longer yourself but to move in an entire universe of your own creating. Today, for instance, as man and woman, both lover and mistress, I rode in a forest on an autumn afternoon under the yellow leaves, and I was also the horses, the leaves, the wind, the words my people uttered, even the red sun that made them almost close their love-drowned eyes. When I brood over these marvelous pleasures I have enjoyed, I would be tempted to offer God a prayer of thanks if I knew he could hear me. Praised may he be for not creating me a cotton merchant, a vaudevillian, or a wit. *Gustave Flaubert (1821–1880)*

224

I'm a lousy writer; a helluva lot of people have got lousy
taste. *Grace Metalious (1924–1964)*

225

A custom loathsome to the eye, hateful to the nose, harmful
to the brain, dangerous to the lungs, and in the black, stinking
fumes thereof, nearest resembling the horrible Stygian smoke
of the pit that is bottomless. *King James (c. 1604) on smoking*

226

I can write better than anybody who can write faster, and I can
write faster than anybody who can write better.
A. J. Liebling (1904–1963)

227

I used to be treated like an idiot, now I'm treated like an idiot savant.

> *Martin Cruz Smith after his novel*
> Gorky Park *became a best-seller*

228

Income tax returns are the most imaginative fiction being written today.   *Herman Wouk*

229

Marry money.   *Max Shulman's advice to aspiring authors*

230

What is a writer but a shmuck with an Underwood?

> *Jack Warner* (*ascribed*)

231

There's no thief like a bad book.   *Italian proverb*

232

A big book is a big bore.   *Callimachus* (*c. 260* B.C.)

Never read a book that is not a year old.
Ralph Waldo Emerson (1803–1882)

The man who doesn't read good books has no advantage over the man who can't read them.   *Mark Twain (1835–1910)*

Any ordinary man can . . . surround himself with two thousand books . . . and thenceforward have at least one place in the world in which it is possible to be happy.
Augustine Birrell (1850–1933)

I have always imagined that Paradise will be a kind of library.   *Jorge Luis Borges*

Studying literature at Harvard is like learning about women at the Mayo Clinic.   *Roy Blount, Jr.*

I wonder how so insupportable a thing as a bookseller was ever permitted to grow up in the Commonwealth. Many of our modern booksellers are but needless excrements, or rather vermin.   *George Wither (1588–1667)*

239

It takes the publishing industry so long to produce books it's no wonder so many are posthumous.   *Teressa Skelton*

240

In every fat book there is a thin book trying to get out.   *Unknown*

241

No, I haven't read the New Testament, but I read the Old Testament, and I liked it very, very much.
One shepherd to another in a New Yorker *cartoon*

242

What an ugly beast is the ape, and how like us.
Cicero (106—43 B.C.*)*

Your life story would not make a good book. Don't even try. *Fran Liebowitz*

Drunkenness is the ruin of reason. It is premature old age. It is temporary death. *St. Basil (330?–379?)*

I drink no more than a sponge. *Rabelais (1494–1553)*

They talk of my drinking but never my thirst.

Scottish proverb

A drinker has a hole under his nose that all his money runs into. *Thomas Fuller (1608–1661)*

'Twas a woman who drove me to drink, and I never had the courtesy to thank her for it. *W. C. Fields (1880–1946)*

An Irishman is the only man in the world who will step over the bodies of a dozen naked women to get to a bottle of stout.   *Unknown*

250

One more drink and I'll be under the host.
Dorothy Parker (1893–1967)

251

I drink to make other people more interesting.
George Jean Nathan (1882–1958)

252

Inflation has gone up over a dollar a quart.
W. C. Fields (1880–1946)

253

Even though a number of people have tried, no one has yet found a way to drink for a living.   *Jean Kerr*

254

I haven't touched a drop of alcohol since the invention of the funnel. *Malachy McCourt*

255

The less I behave like Whistler's mother the night before, the more I look like her the morning after.

Tallulah Bankhead (1903–1968)

256

One reason I don't drink is that I want to know when I am having a good time. *Nancy, Lady Astor (1879–1964)*

257

I'd rather have a free bottle in front of me than a prefrontal lobotomy. *Unknown*

258

I hate to advocate drugs, alcohol, violence, or insanity to anyone, but they've always worked for me.

Hunter S. Thompson

259

If you drink, don't drive. Don't even putt. *Dean Martin*

260

I tremble for my country when I reflect that God is just.
Thomas Jefferson (1743–1826)

261

If you weren't such a great man you'd be a terrible bore.
Mrs. William Gladstone to her husband

262

He speaks to me as if I were a public meeting.
Queen Victoria (1819–1901) on Gladstone

263

Harding was not a bad man, he was just a slob.
Alice Roosevelt Longworth (1884–1980)

264

The only man, woman, or child who ever wrote a simple
declarative sentence with seven grammatical errors is dead.
*e. e. cummings (1894–1962) on the death of
Warren G. Harding, 1923*

265

In 1932, lame duck President Herbert Hoover was so desperate
to remain in the White House that he dressed up as Eleanor
Roosevelt. When FDR discovered the hoax in 1936, the two
men decided to stay together for the sake of the children.
Johnny Carson

The Arabs are a backward people who eat nothing but camel dung. *Winston Churchill (1874–1965)*

Things have never been more like the way they are today in history. *Dwight David Eisenhower (1890–1969)*

John Foster Dulles.
> *Mort Sahl on being asked to say something funny*

Listen, there is no courage or any extra courage that I know of to find out the right thing to do. Now, it is not only necessary to do the right thing, but to do it in the right way and the only problem you have is what is the right thing to do and what is the right way to do it. That is the problem. But this economy of ours is not so simple that it obeys to the opinion of bias or the pronouncements of any particular individual, even to the President. This is an economy that is made up of 173 million people and it reflects their desires, they're ready to buy, they're to spend, it is a thing that is too complex and too big to be affected adversely or advantageously just by a few words or any particular—say, a little this and that, or even a panacea so alleged.

> *Dwight David Eisenhower (1890–1969) in response to the question: "Has government been lacking in courage and boldness in facing up to the recession?"*

Nixon is a shifty-eyed goddamn liar. . . . He's one of the few in the history of this country to run for high office talking out of both sides of his mouth at the same time and lying out of both sides.

Harry S. Truman (1884–1972)

271

I don't give a shit about the Italian lira.
President Richard M. Nixon on being asked by H. R. Haldeman if he wanted to hear a report on the decline of the Italian lira.

272

I would have made a good Pope. *Richard M. Nixon*

273

How do you like that guy? Can't run six balls and he's President of the United States. *Pool hustler Johnny Irish on Nixon*

274

Henry Kissinger may have wished I had presented him as a combination of Charles DeGaulle and Disraeli, but I didn't . . . out of respect for DeGaulle and Disraeli. I described him as a cowboy because that is how he described himself. If I were a cowboy I would be offended. *Oriana Fallaci*

275

Jerry Ford is a nice guy, but he played too much football with his helmet off.   *Lyndon Baines Johnson (1908–1973)*

276

I never trust a man unless I've got his pecker in my pocket.   *Lyndon Baines Johnson (1908–1973)*

277

No.

President Jimmy Carter's daughter Amy when asked by a reporter if she had any message for the children of America.

278

Sometimes when I look at my children I say to myself, "Lillian, you should have stayed a virgin."

Lillian Carter, mother of Jimmy and Billy

279

"Who's Virginia?"

Rose Kennedy when asked why her daughter-in-law Joan lived in Boston while her son Ted lived in Virginia.

I see the world in very fluid, contradictory, emerging, inter-connected terms, and with that kind of circuitry I just don't feel the need to say what is going to happen or will not happen.
California Governor Jerry Brown

Ronald Reagan is not a typical politician because he doesn't know how to lie, cheat, and steal. He's always had an agent for that. *Bob Hope*

Ronald Reagan is the Fred Astaire of foot-in-mouth disease. *Jeff Davis*

Never forget that the most powerful force on earth is love.
Nelson Rockefeller (1908–1979) to Henry Kissinger

Sure Reagan promised to take senility tests. But what if he forgets? *Lorna Kerr-Walker*

Ronald Reagan is the most ignorant president since Warren Harding. *Ralph Nader*

286

Ronald Reagan has held the two most demeaning jobs in the country—President of the United States and radio broadcaster for the Chicago Cubs.   *George Will*

287

Nancy Reagan fell down and broke her hair.

Johnny Carson

288

Well, I would—if they realized that we—again if—if we led them back to that stalemate only because that our retaliatory power, our seconds, or strike at them after our first strike, would be so destructive that they couldn't afford it, that would hold them off.   *Ronald Reagan when asked if nuclear war could be limited to tactical weapons.*

289

Nixon, Ford, Carter, Reagan—a Mount Rushmore of incompetence.   *David Steinberg*

290

When I was a boy I was told that anybody could become President; I'm beginning to believe it.

Clarence Darrow (1857–1938)

291

I'd rather entrust the government of the United States to the first 400 people listed in the Boston telephone directory than to the faculty of Harvard University.

William F. Buckley, Jr.

292

The only thing that saves us from the bureaucracy is its inefficiency. *Eugene McCarthy*

293

We have a crisis of leadership in this country. Where are the Washingtons, the Jeffersons, and the Jacksons? I'll tell you where they are—they are playing professional football and basketball. *Unknown*

294

It is inaccurate to say I hate everything. I am strongly in favor of common sense, common honesty, and common decency. This makes me forever ineligible for any public office.

H. L. Mencken (1880–1956)

295

What this country needs is more unemployed politicians.

Edward Langley

296

All right, I will learn to read, but when I have learned, I never, never shall.
British novelist David Garnett
at age 4, to his mother

297

Henry James writes fiction as if it were a painful duty.
Oscar Wilde (1854–1900)

298

Henry James chews more than he bites off.
Mrs. Henry Adams (c. 1880)

299

Henry James was one of the nicest old ladies I ever met.
William Faulkner (1897–1962)

300

Henry James would have been vastly improved as a novelist by a few whiffs of the Chicago stockyards.
H. L. Mencken (1880–1956)

301

Henry James created more convincing women than Iris Murdoch put together.   *Wilfred Sheed*

302

Go not in and out of court that thy name may not stink.
The Wisdom of Anii (c. 900 B.C.)

303

A lawyer and a wagon-wheel must be well greased.
German proverb

304

Law is a bottomless pit.
John Arbuthnot (1667–1735) (c. 1712)

305

Lawyers, I suppose, were children once.
Charles Lamb (1775–1834)

306

When men are pure, laws are useless; when men are corrupt,
laws are broken. *Benjamin Disraeli (1804–1881)*

307

I became a policeman because I wanted to be in a business
where the customer is always wrong.
Unnamed officer quoted by Arlene Heath

308

The mistakes are all there waiting to be made.
Chessmaster Savielly Grigorievitch Tartakower
(1887–1956) on the game's opening position.

Moral victories don't count.
Savielly Grigorievitch Tartakower (1887–1956)

310

The only reason I would take up jogging is so that I could hear heavy breathing again. *Erma Bombeck*

311
I don't jog. If I die I want to be sick. *Abe Lemons*

312

It was such a primitive country we didn't even see any joggers. *Hamilton cartoon caption*

313

Be careful about reading health books. You may die of a misprint. *Mark Twain (1835–1910)*

314

Old people shouldn't eat health foods. They need all the preservatives they can get. *Robert Orben*

315

A closed mouth gathers no feet. *Unknown*

PART TWO

Miscellaneous

316

Never eat more than you can lift.   *Miss Piggy*

317

Punctuality is the thief of time.   *Oscar Wilde (1854–1900)*

318

Platitudes are the Sundays of stupidity.   *Unknown*

319

It is unbecoming for young men to utter maxims.
Aristotle (384–322 B.C.)

320

They were such a progressive couple they tried to adopt a gay baby.   *Unknown*

321

He who marries a widow will often have a dead man's head thrown in his dish.   *Spanish proverb*

322

I don't know the key to success, but the key to failure is trying to please everybody.   *Bill Cosby*

323

The brain is a wonderful organ; it starts working the moment you get up in the morning and does not stop until you get to the office.   *Robert Frost (1874–1963)*

324

I have never seen a greater monster or miracle than myself.   *Montaigne (1533–1592)*

325

Until you walk a mile in another man's moccasins you can't imagine the smell.   *RB*

326

I don't have a warm personal enemy left. They've all died off. I miss them terribly because they helped define me.
Claire Boothe Luce

327

I'm lonesome. They are all dying. I have hardly a warm personal enemy left.   *James McNeill Whistler (1834–1903)*

328

Nothing is said that has not been said before.
Terence (185–159 B.C.)

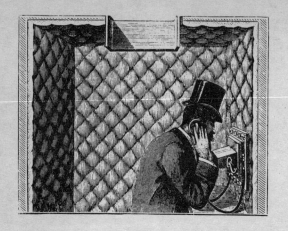

329

I'm in a phone booth at the corner of Walk and Don't Walk. *Unknown*

330

How come they picked you to be an astronaut? You got such a great sense of direction? *Jackie Mason*

331

Recipe (in its entirety) for boiled owl:
Take feathers off. Clean owl and put in cooking pot with lots of water. Add salt to taste. The Eskimo Cookbook (*1952*)

332

Do not make loon soup.
Valuable advice from The Eskimo Cookbook

333

Fall is my favorite season in Los Angeles, watching the birds change color and fall from the trees.   *David Letterman*

334

I met a guy once who was half Italian and half Chinese. His name was Video Pong.   *Unknown*

335

My father never lived to see his dream come true of an all-Yiddish-speaking Canada.   *David Steinberg*

336

That man has missed something who has never left a brothel at sunrise feeling like throwing himself into the river out of pure disgust.   *Gustave Flaubert (1821–1880)*

337

Gary Cooper and Greta Garbo may be the same person. Have you ever seen them together?   *Ernst Lubitsch (1892–1947)*

338

He had a God-given killer instinct.
            Al Davis of the Oakland Raiders on George Blanda

I was gratified to be able to answer promptly. I said I don't know.   *Mark Twain (1835–1910)*

Few people know how to be old.

La Rochefoucauld (1613–1680)

The enemy came. He was beaten. I am tired. Goodnight.
*Message sent by Vicomte Turenne after the battle of
Dunen, 1658*

Byrne's Law: In any electrical circuit, appliances and wiring will burn out to protect fuses.   *RB*

McCabe's Law: Nobody *has* to do *anything*.

Charles McCabe

Parker's Law: Beauty is only skin deep, but ugly goes clear to the bone.   *from* Murphy's Law

Chamberlain's Law: Everything tastes more or less like chicken.   *from* The Official Rules

346

A man can wear a hat for years without being oppressed by
its shabbiness.   *James Douglas*

347

Boozer's Revision: A bird in the hand is dead.
                                        from The Official Rules

348

Any fool can make a rule.
                              Henry David Thoreau (1817–1862)

349

Happiness Is Seeing Lubbock, Texas, in the Rearview Mirror. *Song title*

350

The important thing in acting is to be able to laugh and cry. If I have to cry, I think of my sex life. If I have to laugh, I think of my sex life. *Glenda Jackson*

351

There are more bores around than when I was a boy.
Fred Allen (1894–1956)

352

I've tried relaxing, but—I don't know—I feel more comfortable tense. *Hamilton cartoon caption*

353

I'm just a person trapped inside a woman's body.
Elaine Boosler

354

I happened to catch my reflection the other day when I was polishing my trophies, and, gee, it's easy to see why women are nuts about me. *Tom Ryan*

355

What to do in case of emergency:
1. Pick up your hat
2. Grab your coat
3. Leave your worries on the doorstep
4. Direct your feet to the sunny side of the street.

Unknown

356

Nolan Ryan is pitching much better now that he has his curve ball straightened out.   *Joe Garagiola*

357

In many ways the saying "Know thyself" is lacking. Better to know other people.   *Menander (342?–292? B.C.)*

358

Only the shallow know themselves.

Oscar Wilde (1854–1900)

359

We all have the strength to endure the misfortunes of others.   *La Rochefoucauld (1613–1680)*

360

There is no sweeter sound than the crumbling of one's fellow man.   *Groucho Marx (1890–1977)*

361

It takes a great man to make a good listener.
Arthur Helps (1813–1875)

362

In this business you either sink or swim or you don't.
David Smith

363

I don't have a photograph, but you can have my footprints.
They're upstairs in my socks. *Groucho Marx (1890–1977)*

364

I've always been interested in people, but I've never liked them.   *Somerset Maugham (1874–1965)*

365

Are you going to come quietly or do I have to use ear-plugs?   *From* The Goon Show

366

One of the symptoms of an approaching nervous breakdown is the belief that one's work is terribly important.
Bertrand Russell (1872–1970)

367

A little inaccuracy sometimes saves tons of explanation.
H. H. Munro (Saki) (1870–1916)

368

It's really hard to be roommates with people if your suitcases are much better than theirs.   *J. D. Salinger*

369

Take most people, they're crazy about cars. I'd rather have a goddamn horse. A horse is at least *human*, for God's sake.   *J. D. Salinger*

370

Three o'clock is always too late or too early for anything you want to do.   *Jean-Paul Sartre (1905–1980)*

371

A reformer is a guy who rides through a sewer in a glass-bottomed boat.

New York Mayor Jimmy Walker (1881–1946) in 1928

372

The doctor can bury his mistakes but an architect can only advise his client to plant vines.

Frank Lloyd Wright (1869–1959)

373

I wash everything on the gentle cycle. It's much more humane. *Unknown.*

374

The breakfast of champions is not cereal, it's the opposition. *Nick Seitz*

375

There is nothing in the world so enjoyable as a thorough-going monomania. *Agnes Repplier (1858–1950)*

376

Virtue is its own revenge. *E. Y. Harburg (1898–1981)*

377

A good deed never goes unpunished. *Gore Vidal*

378

The curtain rises on a vast primitive wasteland, not unlike
certain parts of New Jersey. *Woody Allen*

379

Man is the only animal that laughs and has a state legislature. *Samuel Butler (1835–1902)*

380

Until a child is one year old it is incapable of sin.
The Talmud (c. 200)

381

I wish people who have trouble communicating would just shut up. *Tom Lehrer*

382

A man is as young as the woman he feels.
Variously ascribed

383

Toots Shor's restaurant is so crowded nobody goes there anymore. *Yogi Berra*

384

I don't care what is written about me so long as it isn't true. *Dorothy Parker (1893–1967)*

385

He can beat yourn with hisn and he can beat hisn with yourn.
Pro football coach "Bum" Phillips on the merits of coach Don Shula

386

More than any time in history mankind faces a cross[?]
path leads to despair and utter hopelessness, the othe[?]
extinction. Let us pray that we have the wisdom to [?]se
correctly.   *Woody Allen*

387

It is dangerous to be sincere unless you are also stupid.
                    George Bernard Shaw (1856–1950)

388

You can't steal second base and keep one foot on first.
                    An unnamed 60-year-old junior executive

389

When something good happens it's a miracle and you should
wonder what God is saving up for you later.
                    Marshall Brickman

390

Cogito ergo spud. I think, therefore I yam.   *Graffito*

391

If you want an audience, start a fight.   *Gaelic proverb*

392

Everything hurts.   *Michaelangelo Antonioni*

I propose getting rid of conventional armaments and replacing them with reasonably priced hydrogen bombs that would be distributed equally throughout the world. *Idi Amin*

394

I like a woman with a head on her shoulders. I hate necks.
                                                    Steve Martin

395

I don't know why people like the home run so much. A home run is over as soon as it starts . . . wham, bam, thank you, ma'am. The triple is the most exciting play of the game. A triple is like meeting a woman who excites you, spending the evening talking and getting more excited, then taking her home. It drags on and on. You're never sure how it's going to turn out.   *Baseball player George Foster*

396

Working on television is like being shot out of a cannon. They cram you all up with rehearsals, then someone lights a fuse and—BANG—there you are in someone's living room.
Tallulah Bankhead (1903–1968)

397

Talk is cheap because supply exceeds demand.   *Unknown*

398

Fifteen cents of every twenty-cent stamp goes for storage.
Louis Rukeyser

399

The unique thing about Margaret Rutherford is that she can act with her chin alone. Among its many moods I especially cherish the chin commanding, the chin in doubt, and the chin at bay.   *Kenneth Tynan*

400

Things are so bad on Broadway today an actor is lucky to be miscast.   *George S. Kaufman (1889–1961)*

401

The race may not be to the swift nor the victory to the strong, but that's how you bet.   *Damon Runyon (1844–1946)*

402

The Jewish position on abortion is that a foetus is a foetus until it gets out of medical school.   *Unknown*

403

I'm impressed with people from Chicago. Hollywood is hype, New York is talk, Chicago is work.
Actor-producer Michael Douglas

404

An empty taxi stopped, and Jack Warner got out.   *Unknown*

405

A liberated woman is one who has sex before marriage and a job after.   *Gloria Steinem*

406

If you haven't got anything nice to say about anybody, come sit next to me.   *Alice Roosevelt Longworth (1884–1980)*

407

I'll try anything once.
Alice Roosevelt Longworth (1884–1980) on giving birth at age 41.

408

Days off.   *Spencer Tracy (1900–1967) when asked what he looks for in a script.*

409

We are drawn to our television sets each April the way we are drawn to the scene of an accident.
Vincent Canby on the Academy Awards

410

God sends meat and the devil sends cooks.
Thomas Deloney (1543–1600)

411

Husbands are like fires. They go out if unattended.
Zsa Zsa Gabor (Miss Hungary of 1936)

412

Go, and never darken my towels again.

Groucho Marx (1895–1977)

413

California is the only state in the union where you can fall asleep under a rose bush in full bloom and freeze to death.   *W. C. Fields (1880–1946)*

414

The difference between Los Angeles and yoghurt is that yoghurt has an active, living culture.   *Unknown*

415

We can see California coming, and we're scared.
James Brady

416

Many a man owes his success to his first wife and his second wife to his success.   *Jim Backus*

417

Nature has given us two ears but only one mouth.
Benjamin Disraeli (1804–1881)

418

It is easier to stay out than get out.
Mark Twain (1835–1910)

419

A fat paunch never breeds fine thoughts.
St. Jerome (340?–420))

Absence makes the heart go yonder. *RB*

Short, balding, Chinese gentleman seeks tall Negress with passion for leather and Brahms to attend openings.

Classified ad in the Berkeley Barb

Yard sale—Recently married couple is combining households. All duplicates will be sold, except children.

Classified ad in the San Jose Mercury News

It takes two to speak the truth—one to speak and another to hear. *Henry David Thoreau (1817–1862)*

Only sick music makes money today.

Nietzsche (1844–1900) in 1888

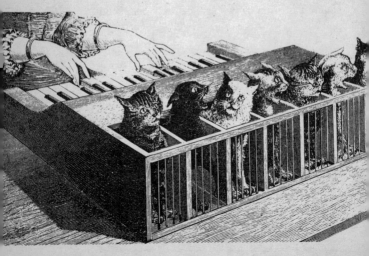

425

I never know how much of what I say is true.   *Bette Midler*

426

I'm as pure as the driven slush.
                              Tallulah Bankhead (1903–1968)

427

I went around the world last year and you want to know something? It hates each other.   *Edward J. Mannix*

428

A great many people have come up to me and asked how I managed to get so much done and still look so dissipated.   *Robert Benchley (1889–1945)*

429

I don't trust him. We're friends.
                              Bertolt Brecht (1898–1956)

430

A man can't be too careful in the choice of his enemies.
                              Oscar Wilde (1854–1900)

431

Anyone can win, unless there happens to be a second entry.   *George Ade (1866–1944)*

We have long passed the Victorian era, when asterisks were followed after a certain interval by a baby.
Somerset Maugham (1874–1965)

It was such a lovely day I thought it was a pity to get up. *Somerset Maugham (1874–1965)*

The biggest sin is sitting on your ass. *Florynce Kennedy*

Laugh and the world laughs with you, snore and you sleep alone. *Anthony Burgess*

It was a blonde, a blonde to make a bishop kick a hole in a stained glass window. *Raymond Chandler (1888–1959)*

I go to the theater to be entertained . . . I don't want to see rape, sodomy, and drug addiction. I can get all that at home.
Roger Law cartoon caption

The higher the buildings, the lower the morals.
Noel Coward (1899–1973)

439

Nothing is illegal if a hundred businessmen decide to do it.   *Andrew Young*

440

I wish Frank Sinatra would just shut up and sing.

Lauren Bacall

441

England produces the best fat actors.

Jimmy Cannon (1910–1973)

442

If it weren't for Philo T. Farnsworth, inventor of television, we'd still be eating frozen radio dinners.

Johnny Carson

443

A luxury liner is just a bad play surrounded by water.

Clive James

444

The future isn't what it used to be.   *Variously ascribed*

445

Some of us are becoming the men we wanted to marry.

Gloria Steinem

446

I haven't been wrong since 1961, when I thought I made a mistake.   *Bob Hudson*

447

I may have my faults, but being wrong ain't one of them.

Jimmy Hoffa (1913–1975)

448

He had a winning smile, but everything else was a loser.

George C. Scott at a Bob Hope roast

449

He not only overflowed with learning, he stood in the slop.
Sydney Smith (1771–1845) on Macaulay

450

Listening to the Fifth Symphony of Ralph Vaughan Williams
is like staring at a cow for forty-five minutes.   *Aaron Copland*

451

Forgive your enemies, but never forget their names.
John F. Kennedy (1917–1963)

452

There is no pleasure in having nothing to do; the fun is having
lots to do and not doing it.   *John W. Raper*

453

Hope is the feeling you have that the feeling you have isn't
permanent.   *Jean Kerr*

454

I was probably the only revolutionary ever referred to as
"cute."   *Abbie Hoffman*

455

Success didn't spoil me; I've always been insufferable.
Fran Liebowitz

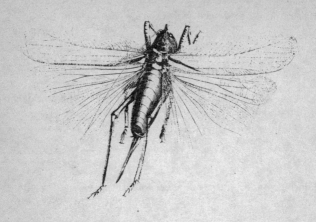

456

Men should stop fighting among themselves and start fighting insects.   *Luther Burbank (1849–1926)*

457

They say you can't do it, but sometimes it doesn't always work.   *Casey Stengel (1891–1975)*

458

Tumescence is the period between pubescence and senescence.   *RB*

459

If this is coffee, please bring me some tea; but if this is tea, please bring me some coffee.

Abraham Lincoln (1809–1865)

460

Logic is in the eye of the logician.   *Gloria Steinem*

461

Everything is in a state of flux, including the status quo.

RB

462

The only people with a right to complain about what I do for a living are vegetarian nudists.

*Ken Bates, one of California's
700 licensed fur trappers*

463

I'm trying to arrange my life so that I don't even have to be present.   *Unknown*

464

To travel is to discover that everyone is wrong about other countries.   *Aldous Huxley (1894–1963)*

465

It can be great fun to have an affair with a bitch.

Louis Auchincloss

466

Never accept a drink from a urologist.

Erma Bombeck's father

467

In Rome I am weighed down by a lack of momentum, the inertia of a spent civilization. In New York I feel plugged into a strong alternating current of hope and despair.   *Ted Morgan*

468

I'm six foot eleven. My birthday covers three days.
Darryl Dawkins

469

He who hesitates is not only lost, but miles from the next exit.   *Unknown*

470

You can't measure time in days the way you can money in dollars because every day is different.   *Jorge Luis Borges*

471

Time is nature's way of keeping everything from happening at once.   *Unknown*

472

If Today Was a Fish, I'd Throw It Back In.   *Song title*

473

From the Gutter to You Ain't Up.   *Song title*

474

I look at ordinary people in their suits, them with no scars, and I'm different. I don't fit with them. I'm where everybody's got scar tissue on their eyes and got noses like saddles. I go to conventions of old fighters like me and I see the scar tissue and all them flat noses and it's beautiful. Galento, may he rest in peace. Giardello, LaMotta, Carmen Basilio. What a sweetheart Basilio is. They talk like me, like they got rocks in their throats. Beautiful!   *Willie Pastrano*

475

Reality is a crutch for people who can't cope with drugs.
                                        Lily Tomlin

A cap of good acid costs five dollars and for that you can hear
the Universal Symphony with God singing solo and the Holy
Ghost on drums.

> *Hunter S. Thompson as quoted by William F.*
> *Buckley, Jr., who added: "Though one should be*
> *prepared to vomit rather frequently and disport*
> *with pink elephants and assorted grotesqueries*
> *while trying, often unsuccessfully, to make one's*
> *way to the toilet."*

The best way to lose weight is to get the flu and take a trip to
Egypt.　*Roz Lawrence*

Anyone who eats three meals a day should understand why
cookbooks outsell sex books three to one.　*L. M. Boyd*

We don't know a millionth of one percent about anything.　*Thomas Alva Edison (1847–1931)*

Something ignoble, loathsome, undignified attends all asso-
ciations between people and has been transferred to all objects,
dwellings, tools, even the landscape itself.

> *Bertolt Brecht (1898–1956) on America*

481

If I had known I was going to live this long I would have taken better care of myself.   *Unknown*

482

Is sloppiness in speech caused by ignorance or apathy? I don't know and I don't care.   *William Safire*

483

We had seen the light at the end of the tunnel, and it was out. *John C. Clancy*

484

To err is human, to forgive supine.
                                    S. J. Perelman (1904–1979)

485

What is true is what I can't help believing.
                        Oliver Wendell Holmes, Jr. (1841–1935)

486

I am the last of Britain's stately homos.

                                            Quentin Crisp

487

I didn't want to be rich, I just wanted enough to get the couch reupholstered. *Kate (Mrs. Zero) Mostel*

488

My father and he had one of those English friendships which begin by avoiding intimacies and eventually eliminate speech altogether. *Jorge Luis Borges*

489

Shut up he explained. *Ring Lardner (1885–1933)*

490

She had two complexions, A.M. and P.M.

Ring Lardner (1885–1933)

491

He writes so well he makes me feel like putting my quill back in my goose.   *Fred Allen (1894–1956)*

492

If my film makes one more person miserable, I'll feel I've done my job.   *Woody Allen*

493

The cloning of humans is on most of the lists of things to worry about from Science, along with behavior control, genetic engineering, transplanted heads, computer poetry and the unrestrained growth of plastic flowers.   *Lewis Thomas*

494

No one can earn a million dollars honestly.

William Jennings Bryan (1860–1925)

495

There are very few Japanese Jews. As a result, there is no Japanese word for Alan King.   *Johnny Carson*

From birth to age 18, a girl needs good parents, from 18 to 35 she needs good looks, from 35 to 55 she needs a good personality, and from 55 on she needs cash.

Sophie Tucker (1884?–1966)

497

Outer space is no place for a person of breeding.

Lady Violet Bonham Carter (1887–1969)

498

Our national flower is the concrete cloverleaf.

Lewis Mumford

499

The only normal people are the ones you don't know very well. *Joe Ancis*

500

You sofa-crevice fondler! *Peter De Vries*

501

Cats are like Baptists. They raise hell but you can't catch them at it. *Unknown*

502

So little time and so little to do.

Oscar Levant (1906–1972)

503

It's a rare person who wants to hear what he doesn't want to hear. *Dick Cavett*

504

When I hear the word "culture" I reach for my gun.

Hans Johst (c. 1939)

505

He washed his legs today and can't do a thing with them.
Sportscaster Lon Simmons on seeing a baseball player fall down twice in the first inning

506

I like men to behave like men—strong and childish.
Françoise Sagan

507

A kleptomaniac is a person who helps himself because he can't help himself.   *Henry Morgan*

508

A hypocrite is a person who—but who isn't?
Don Marquis (1878–1937)

509

Brain damage reading test:
   People tell me one thing and out the other. I feel as much like I did yesterday as I did today. I never liked room temperature. My throat is closer than it seems. Likes and dislikes are among my favorites. No napkin is sanitary enough for me. I don't like any of my loved ones.   *Daniel M. Wegner*

510

The two hardest things to handle in life are failure and success.   *Unknown*

511

Progress might have been all right once but it has gone on too long. *Ogden Nash (1902–1971)*

512

I consider exercise vulgar. It makes people smell.
Alec Yuill Thornton

513

There is no human problem which could not be solved if people would simply do as I advise.   *Gore Vidal*

514

What's on your mind, if you will allow the overstatement?
Fred Allen (1894–1956)

515

The young man who has not wept is a savage, and the old man who will not laugh is a fool.
George Santayana (1866–1952)

516

Though I am not naturally honest, I am so sometimes by chance.   *Shakespeare (1564–1616)*

517

Early to rise and early to bed makes a male healthy, wealthy and dead.   *James Thurber (1894–1961)*

518

I have no relish for the country; it is a kind of healthy grave.   *Sydney Smith (1771–1845)*

519

A farm is an irregular patch of nettles, bound by short term notes, containing a fool and his wife who didn't know enough to stay in the city.   *S. J. Perelman (1904–1979)*

520

Everything has been figured out except how to live.

Jean-Paul Sartre (1905–1980)

521

Howard Hughes was able to afford the luxury of madness, like a man who not only thinks he is Napoleon but hires an army to prove it.   *Ted Morgan*

522

When it is not necessary to make a decision, it is necessary not to make a decision.   *Lord Falkland (1610?–1643)*

523

This book fills a much-needed gap.

Moses Hadas (1900–1966) in a review

524

Thank you for sending me a copy of your book. I'll waste no time reading it.   *Moses Hadas (1900–1966) in a letter*

525

There are plenty of good five-cent cigars in the country. The trouble is they cost a quarter. What this country really needs is a good five-cent nickel.   *Franklin P. Adams (1881–1960)*

526

Being perfectly well-dressed gives a feeling of tranquility that religion is powerless to bestow.

Ralph Waldo Emerson (1803–1882),
quoting a friend

527

We are here and it is now. Further than that all human knowledge is moonshine.   *H. L. Mencken (1880–1956)*

528

There is no kind of dishonesty into which otherwise good people more easily and frequently fall than that of defrauding the government.   *Benjamin Franklin (1706–1790)*

529

Don't get the idea that I'm knocking the American system.
Al Capone (1899–1947)

530

It wasn't raining when Noah built the ark.   *Howard Ruff*

531

The learned are seldom pretty fellows, and in many cases their appearance tends to discourage a love of study in the young.   *H. L. Mencken (1880–1956)*

532

There is something going on now in Mexico that I happen to think is cruelty to animals. What I'm talking about, of course, is cat juggling.   *Steve Martin*

533

Truth is beautiful, without doubt; but so are lies.

Ralph Waldo Emerson (1803–1882)

534

We will march forward to a better tomorrow so long as separate groups like the blacks, the Negroes, and the coloreds can come together to work out their differences.

Steve Allen at a Redd Foxx roast

535

Ninety-eight percent of the adults in this country are decent, hard-working, honest Americans. It's the other lousy two percent that get all the publicity. But then—we elected them.

Lily Tomlin

536

There are more of them than us.   *Herb Caen*

537

Suppose you were an idiot and suppose you were a member of Congress. But I repeat myself.   *Mark Twain (1835–1910)*

538

Never go to bed mad. Stay up and fight.   *Phyllis Diller*

539

When I got to the beauty parlor, I always use the emergency entrance. Sometimes I just go for an estimate.   *Phyllis Diller*

540

Orthodox medicine has not found an answer to your complaint. However, luckily for you, I happen to be a quack.

Richter cartoon caption

541

One of a hostess's duties is to act as a procuress.

Marcel Proust (1871–1922)

542

Here is a supplementary bulletin from the Office of Fluctuation Control, Bureau of Edible Condiments, Soluble and Indigestible Fats and Glutinous Derivatives, Washington, D.C. Correction of Directive 943456201, issued a while back, concerning the fixed price of groundhog meat. In the directive above named, the quotation on groundhog meat should read ground hog-meat.   *Bob and Ray*

543

I've known what it is to be hungry, but I always went right to a restaurant.   *Ring Lardner (1885–1933)*

544

What dreadful hot weather we have! It keeps me in a continual state of inelegance. *Jane Austen (1775–1817)*

545

A single sentence will suffice for modern man: He fornicated and read the papers. *Albert Camus (1913–1960)*

546

The rich are the scum of the earth in every country.
G. K. Chesterton (1874–1936)

547

One should never know too precisely whom one has married. *Nietzsche (1844–1900) on* Lohengrin

548

I never lecture, not because I am shy or a bad speaker, but simply because I detest the sort of people who go to lectures and don't want to meet them. *H. L. Mencken (1880–1956)*

549

Bed is the poor man's opera. *Italian proverb*

550

I'd rather be black than gay because when you're black you don't have to tell your mother. *Charles Pierce*

551

Roses are red, violets are blue,
I'm a schizophrenic, and so am I. *Frank Crow*

552

Lie Down and Roll Over and 159 Other Ways To Say I Love You. *1981 book title*

553

I improve on misquotation. *Cary Grant*

554

Partying is such sweet sorrow. *RB*

555

Honest criticism is hard to take, particularly from a relative, a friend, an acquaintance, or a stranger.   *Franklin P. Jones*

556

If any cleric or monk speaks jocular words, such as provoke laughter, let him be anathema.
Ordinance, Second Council of Constance (1418)

557

Better that a girl has beauty than brains because boys see better than they think.   *Unknown*

558

I talk to myself because I like dealing with a better class of people. *Jackie Mason*

559

It is better to have a permanent income than to be fascinating. *Oscar Wilde (1854 – 1900)*

560

I did not sleep. I never do when I am over-happy, over-unhappy, or in bed with a strange man. *Edna O'Brien*

Dostoyevsky was one of those neurotics who recover their health and even their serenity when disaster at last occurs.

V. S. Pritchett

562

Exit, pursued by a bear.

Stage direction in Shakespeare's
The Winter's Tale (*1611*)

563

¿*Como frijoles?* (Spanish for How have you bean?)

Unknown

564

I don't make jokes. I just watch the government and report the facts.   *Will Rogers (1879–1935)*

565

Even in civilized mankind faint traces of monogamous instinct can be perceived.   *Bertrand Russell (1872–1970)*

566

Things to do in Burbank:
>   1. Go to the Safeway parking lot for the roller skating
>   festival called Holiday on Tar.   *Johnny Carson*

567

I would rather be a coward than brave because people hurt you when you are brave.
> *E. M. Forster (1879–1970) as a small child*

568

One day there will be only five kings left, hearts, spades, diamonds, clubs, and England.
> *King Farouk (1920–1965) after his overthrow by Nasser*

569

When ideas fail, words come in very handy.
> *Goethe (1749–1832)*

570

Music with dinner is an insult both to the cook and the violin-
ist.   *G. K. Chesterton (1874–1936)*

571

The place of the father in the modern suburban family is a very
small one, particularly if he plays golf.
Bertrand Russell (1872–1970)

572

Avarice is the sphincter of the heart.
Matthew Green (c. 1737)

573

It is easier to be gigantic than to be beautiful.
Nietzsche (1844–1900)

574

By the time we've made it, we've had it.   *Malcolm Forbes*

575

I only like two kinds of men: domestic and foreign.
Mae West (1893–1980)

576

Where but in Kenya can a man whose grandfather was a cannibal
watch a really good game of polo?
Marina Sulzberger (1920–1976)

577

France was a long despotism tempered by epigrams.
Thomas Carlyle (1759–1881)

578

Never trust anyone over-dirty.   *RB*

579

There are more pleasant things to do than beat up people.

*Muhammad Ali on the occasion of
one of his retirements*

580

Mirrors and copulation are abominable because they increase the numbers of men.   *Jorge Luis Borges*

581

I don't worry about getting old. I'm old already. Only young people worry about getting old. When I was 65 I had cupid's eczema. I don't believe in dying. It's been done. I'm working on a new exit. Besides, I can't die now—I'm booked.

George Burns

582

Men who never get carried away should be.

Malcolm Forbes

583

If you aren't fired with enthusiasm, you will be fired with enthusiasm.   *Vince Lombardi (1913–1970)*

584

When I was kidnapped, my parents snapped into action. They rented out my room.   *Woody Allen*

585

The best cure for hypochondria is to forget about your body and get interested in somebody else's.

Goodman Ace (1899–1982)

586

New invention: Snap-on acne for people who want to look younger.   *Johnny Carson*

587

Love teaches even asses to dance.   *French proverb*

588

Ammonia is beautiful.   *Bumper sticker*

589

FECK OPUC.   *Bumper sticker*

590

There is one fault that I must find
   With the twentieth century,
And I'll put it in a couple of words:
   Too adventury.
What I'd like would be some nice dull monotony
   If anyone's gotony.   *Ogden Nash (1902–1971)*

591

If called by a panther
Don't anther.   *Ogden Nash (1902–1971)*

592

First secure an independent income, then practice virtue.
Greek saying

593

What we call real estate—the solid ground to build a house on—
is the broad foundation on which nearly all of the guilt of the
world rests.   *Nathaniel Hawthorne (1804–1864)*

594

I have never liked working. To me a job is an invasion of pri-
vacy.   *Danny McGoorty (1901–1970)*

595

Boy, the things I do for England.
Prince Charles on sampling snake meat

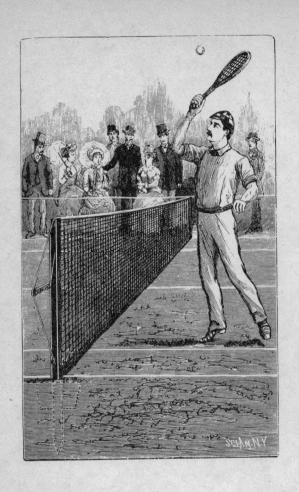

596

Victory goes to the player who makes the next-to-last mistake.
Savielly Grigorievitch Tartakower (1887–1956)

597

Of all noises, I think music is the least disagreeable.
Samuel Johnson (1709–1784)

598

One, two, three,
Buckle my shoe.   *Robert Benchley (1889–1945)*

599

It is rather to be chosen than great riches, unless I have omitted
something from the quotation.

Robert Benchley (1889–1945)
in Maxims From the Chinese

600

There must be 500,000 rats in the United States; of course, I am
only speaking from memory.   *Billy Nye (1850–1896)*

601

Newspapermen learn to call a murderer "an alleged murderer"
and the King of England "the alleged King of England" to avoid
libel suits.   *Stephen Leacock (1869–1944)*

602

Lord Ronald said nothing; he flung himself from the room, flung
himself upon his horse and rode madly off in all direc-
tions.   *Stephen Leacock (1869–1944)*

603

I do not take a single newspaper, nor read one a month, and I feel myself infinitely the happier for it.

Thomas Jefferson (1743–1826)

604

Show me a hero and I will write you a tragedy.

F. Scott Fitzgerald (1896–1940)

605

We can't all be heroes because somebody has to sit on the curb and clap as they go by. *Will Rogers (1879–1935)*

606

Some things have to be believed to be seen.

Ralph Hodgson on ESP

607

One of the most astounding cases of clairvoyance is that of the noted Greek psychic Achilles Loudos. Loudos realized that he had unusual powers by the age of ten, when he could lie in bed and, by concentrating, make his father's false teeth jump out of his mouth. *Woody Allen*

608

A cucumber should be well-sliced, dressed with pepper and vinegar, and then thrown out. *Samuel Johnson (1709–1784)*

Middle age is when you've met so many people that every new person you meet reminds you of someone else.

Ogden Nash (1902–1971)

610

Wagner's music is better than it sounds.

Bill Nye (1850–1896)

6 1 1

With those delicate features of his he would have made a pretty woman, and he probably never has.   *Josefa Heifetz*

6 1 2

I don't want any yes-men around me. I want everybody to tell me the truth even if it costs them their jobs.
Samuel Goldwyn (1882–1974)

6 1 3

The advantage of the emotions is that they lead us astray.
Oscar Wilde (1854–1900)

6 1 4

In the first place, God made idiots. That was for practice. Then he made school boards.   *Mark Twain (1835–1910)*

6 1 5

She wears her clothes as if they were thrown on with a pitch-fork.   *Jonathan Swift (1667–1745)*

6 1 6

A man is known by the company he avoids.

Unknown

6 1 7

Underneath this flabby exterior is an enormous lack of charac-ter.   *Oscar Levant (1906–1972)*

618

Nobody roots for Goliath.   *Wilt Chamberlain*

619

He went to Europe as a boy, where in Geneva his father arranged for a prostitute. He was so terrified by the experience that he didn't marry until he was 67 years old.

John Leonard on Borges

620

Keep breathing.   *Sophie Tucker (1884?–1966)*

621

If people don't want to come out to the ball park, nobody's going to stop them.   *Yogi Berra*

622

Tradition is what you resort to when you don't have the time or the money to do it right.   *Kurt Herbert Adler*

623

It is impossible to imagine Goethe or Beethoven being good at billiards or golf.   *H. L. Mencken (1880–1956)*

624

All truths are half-truths.

Alfred North Whitehead (1861–1947)

625

To generalize is to be an idiot.   *William Blake (1757–1827)*

626

If you look like your passport photo, you're too ill to travel.
Will Kommen

627

How can one conceive of a one-party system in a country that
has over 200 varieties of cheese?
Charles de Gaulle (1890–1970)

628

When you have got an elephant by the hind legs and he is trying
to run away, it is best to let him run.
Abraham Lincoln (1809–1865)

629

After three days, fish and guests stink.

John Lyly (1554?–1606)

630

I was born in Australia because my mother wanted me to be near her. *Unknown*

631

I will always cherish the initial misconceptions I had about you. *Unknown*

632

The majority of those who put together collections of verses or epigrams resemble those who eat cherries or oysters; they begin by choosing the best and end by eating everything.

Chamfort (1741–1794)

633

If you were a member of Jesse James's band and people asked you what you were, you wouldn't say, "Well, I'm a desperado." You'd say something like, "I work in banks," or "I've done some railroad work." It took me a long time just to say "I'm a writer." It's really embarrassing. *Roy Blount, Jr.*

634

It takes about ten years to get used to how old you are.

Unknown

635

After all is said and done, more is said than done.   *Unknown*

636

In the end, everything is a gag.

Charlie Chaplin (1889–1977)

637

Science has not yet found a cure for the pun.   *RB*

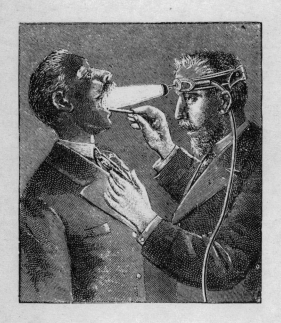

Sources, References, and Notes

Just because this is primarily a book of humor rather than scholarship doesn't mean that credit shouldn't be given where it is due. Unfortunately, my notebooks of "Remarks Worth Remembering" and my memory are spotty on documentation, as are most of the published collections of quotations I have turned to for help. If you know an author or source I failed to give, please write to me in care of the publisher (see Introduction). With help from readers there will be fewer partial and missing ascriptions in the next edition.

I would particularly like to hear from the professional writers of comedy and gags whose handiwork is no doubt credited here and elsewhere to their celebrity clients.

The principal secondary sources I consulted are listed in order of size, each with an identifying letter that will be referred to in the citations that follow.

A. *A New Dictionary of Quotations on Historical Principles*, Selected and edited by H. L. Mencken; Alfred A. Knopf, New York, 1952. (Approximately 37,000 entries)
B. *The Quotable Woman*, Compiled and edited by Elaine Partnow; Anchor Press/Doubleday, New York, 1978. (Approx. 21,000 entries)
C. *Familiar Quotations*, by John Bartlett; Little, Brown, Boston, 1955. (16,000 entries)
D. *The Crown Treasury of Relevant Quotations*, by Edward F. Murphy, Crown Publishers, New York, 1978. (8,000 entries)
E. *The Great Quotations*, Compiled by George Seldes; Lyle Stuart, New York, 1960. (7,000 entries)
F. *Peter's Quotations*, by Laurence J. Peter; William Morrow, New York, 1977. (6,000 entries)
G. *The Hamlyn Pocket Dictionary of Quotations*, Edited by Jonathan Hunt; The Hamlyn Publishing Group, London, 1979. (6,000 entries)

H. *The Penguin Dictionary of Modern Quotations*, J. M. and M. J. Cohen; Penguin Books, Harmondsworth, England, 1976. (5,500 entries)

I. *A Dictionary of Wit, Wisdom & Satire*, by Herbert V. Prochnow and Herbert V. Prochnow, Jr.; Harper & Row, New York, 1962. (5,000 entries)

J. *The Pocket Book of Quotations*, Edited by Henry Davidoff; Pocket Books, New York, 1952. (3,200 entries)

K. *The Book of Quotes*, by Barbara Rowes; E. P. Dutton, New York, 1979. (3,100 entries)

L. *The Quotable Quotations Book*, Compiled by Alec Lewis; Simon & Schuster, New York, 1980. (3,000 entries)

M. *The Viking Book of Aphorisms*, by W. H. Auden and Louis Kronenberger; Viking Press, New York, 1966. (3,000 entries)

N. *Popcorn in Paradise*, *The Wit and Wisdom of Hollywood*, Edited by John Robert Colombo; Holt, Rinehart and Winston, New York, 1980. (3,000 entries)

O. *Nobody Said It Better*, by Miriam Ringo; Rand McNally, Chicago, Ill., 1980. (2,700 entries)

P. *Proverbs and Epigrams*; Ottenheimer Publishers, Baltimore, Md., 1954. (2,500 entries)

Q. *Quotations of Wit and Wisdom*, John W. Gardner and Francesca Gardner Reese; W. W. Norton, New York, 1975. (1,200 entries)

R. *The Book of Insults*, Compiled by Nancy McPhee; St. Martin's Press, New York, 1978. (1,000 entries)

S. *The Writer's Quotation Book*, Edited by James Charlton; Pushcart Press, Yonkers, N.Y., 1980. (350 entries)

Quotation
Number

1. As given in R.

2. "Selections From the Allen Notebooks," in *Without Feathers*, 1975.

5. *Sisyphus*.

6. *Twilight of the Idols*, 1889.

7. *Mackeral Plaza*, 1958.

14. *Anthony Adverse*, 1933.

17. *Soldier, Sage, Saint*, 1978.

18. *One Fat Englishman*, 1963.

19. Possibly a corruption of something Thoreau said about fishing.

21. *The San Francisco Chronicle*, July 20, 1981.
24. *A Certain Slant of Light*, 1980.
25. A "Peanuts" comic strip.
26. As given in L.
27. From a "Peanuts" comic strip, January 1982.
28. *Coop*, 1978.
29. See 270.
30. As given in I.
32. *A Book About Myself*, 1922.
33. As given in M.
34. *The Tragedy of Pudd'nhead Wilson*, 1894.
35. Quoted in *On Being Funny*, by Eric Lax. 1975.
38. *Newsweek*, June 23, 1975.
39. *Seattle Times*.
41. As given in J.
42. *Metropolitan Life*, 1978.
47. *Barrett Wendell and His Letters*, 1924.
49. *The Ginger Man*, 1965.
51. First sentence of the short story *An Imperfect Conflagration*.
52. *Death, A Poem*.
53. *Murder Considered As One of the Fine Arts*, 1827.
54. As given in A. It has been suggested that some of the quotes ascribed to Anonymous in Mencken's great work were written by Mencken himself. This could be one of them.
55. *A Day at the Races*, 1936.
58. Quoted by Anatole Broyard in a *New York Times* book review, 1980.
59. *The San Francisco Chronicle*, June 5, 1981.
60. *The Pushcart Prize V*, 1980.
65. Quoted in *Omni*.
70. *Rhetoric II*.
72. *A Glass Eye at the Keyhole*, 1938.
73–75 *The Devil's Dictionary*, 1906; all have been shortened.
82. *The Devil's Dictionary*, 1906.
83. As quoted in *The San Francisco Chronicle*, April 12, 1981.
84. As given in M.
88. *Notebooks*.
89. *You Don't Have To Be in Who's Who to Know What's What*, 1980.
90. As given in K.
95. *Nature*, 1841.

98. Quoted in *The San Francisco Chronicle*, November 11, 1979.
101. *The Rules of Christian Manners and Civility*, 1695.
105. *Conversations with Gore Vidal*, 1981.
107. As given in B.
108. *Books of the Times*, Vol. II, #7, p. 333.
110. As given in N.
111. *My Early Life*, 1930.
113. Quoted in "The Verbal Karate of Florynce Kennedy," by Gloria Steinem, *Ms.*, March 1973.
114. *Man in the Holocene*, 1980.
121. *Miss Tallulah Bankhead*, by Lee Israel, 1972.
122. *Karl Kraus*, by Harry Zohn, 1980.
124. *Reasons of the Heart*, 1965.
125. *The Most of Malcolm Muggeridge*, 1966.
126. *Vile Bodies*, 1930
129. *Soliloquies I.*
135. As given in Q.
140. As given in Q.
142. *The Picture of Dorian Gray*, 1891.
143. *Reflections of a Bachelor Girl*, 1903.
144. *The Way of All Flesh*, 1903.
147. See 82.
149. As given in A.
150. Quoted by Sara Mayfield in *The Constant Circle*, 1968.
153. Quoted by *The New York Times*, April 29, 1956.
156. Quoted in *Womanlist*, by Weiser and Arbeiter, 1981.
159. Quoted in *Funny People*, by Steve Allen, 1981.
161. TS to RB.
163. From *Happy to Be Here*, 1982. Mr. Keillor uses the third person.
164. Quoted in L. M. Boyd's syndicated newspaper column, *The Grab Bag*.
168. As given in A.
170. As given in E.
174. As given in Q.
175. As given in D.
177. *Don Quixote*, 1605.
179. Sasuly is the author of *Bookies and Bettors*, 1982.
180. Quoted by RB in *McGoorty, The Story of a Billiard Bum*, 1980.
182. Quoted by Charles McCabe in *The San Francisco Chronicle*, June 30, 1978.

186. *The Decline and Fall of Practically Everybody*, 1950.
187. See 186.
188. WH to RB.
196. *Tropic of Cancer*, 1934.
197. As given in I.
198. *Maxims for Revolutionaries*, 1903.
201. *Everybody's Political What's What*.
202. SD is a San Francisco disc jockey.
204. *Legend: Tolstoy's Letters*, 1978.
205. As given in O.
210. As given in Q.
211. In an interview.
217. Quoted by Herbert Mitgang in *The New York Times Book Review*, July 1980.
218. Quoted by William Buckley in *The New York Times Book Review*, April 24, 1977.
219. *New York Times Book Review*, September 16, 1979.
222. As given in S.
223. From his *Journal*.
224. As given in E.
225. As given in E.
226. As recalled by Richard Sasuly (see 179).
230. Also ascribed to others.
238. Slightly shortened.
239. TS to RB.
243. See 42.
247. As given in A.
249. Unnamed "philosopher" quoted by Ron Butler in *San Francisco Examiner*, July 12, 1981.
250. *You Might As Well Live*.
253. *Poor Richard*, Act I, 1963.
254. Quoted in *Variety*.
255. See 150.
256. Quoted in *Reader's Digest*, November 1960.
257. Can anyone identify the creator of this, the greatest spoonerism of all time?
258. Quoted in *Life*, January 1981.
259. As given in K.
263. ARL was Teddy Roosevelt's daughter. For more see *Mrs. L: Conversations with Alice Roosevelt Longworth*, by Michael Teague, 1981.
269. Verbatim transcript, press conference.
270. Quoted by Leo Rosten in *Infinite Riches*, 1978.

271. From the White House tapes.
272. As given in K.
274. Quoted by Jack Anderson, May 1979.
278. Quoted in *Life*. January 1981.
280. In Jeff Davis's column in the *San Francisco Examiner*, October 12, 1980.
284. Quoted by Herb Caen in his *San Francisco Chronicle* column, January 28, 1981.
285. Quoted in *The Pacific Sun*, March 21, 1981.
288. See 269.
290. As given in H.
294. Quoted in *Life*, August 5, 1946.
295. From a letter quoted by Charles McCabe in his *San Francisco Chronicle* column, October 24, 1980.
297. *The Decay of Lying*, 1891.
298. Quoted by Peter De Vries in *The New York Times Book Review*, December 6, 1981.
299. As given in R.
300. *The Smart Set*, November 1920, p. 140.
301. *The Good Word*, 1978.
307. Attorney AH to RB.
311. Quoted by Herb Caen in *The San Francisco Chronicle*, June 1980. AL is the former basketball coach at the University of Texas.
314. RO is a professional gag writer who markets his work to a wide variety of celebrities and politicians, enabling them to feign wit where none exists.
315. Needlepoint sampler recalled by Debi McFarland for RB.
316. *Miss Piggy's Guide to Life*, 1981, by Henry Beard.
317. *The Picture of Dorian Gray*, 1891.
318. As given in Q.
319. *Rhetoric*, c. 322 B.C.
322. As given in K.
323. As given in K.
326. On *The Dick Cavett Show*, July 21, 1981.
327. As given in R.
336. From his *Letters*.
339. *Life on the Mississippi*, 1883.
343. CM is a *San Francisco Chronicle* columnist.
344. *Murphy's Law*, by Arthur Block, 1977.
345. *The Official Rules*, Paul Dickson, 1978.
346. *Down Shoe Lane*.
347. See 345.

348. *Journal*, February 3, 1860.
350. See 164.
361. *Brevia*.
362. As recalled by Charles Champlin.
363. *A Night at the Opera*, 1935.
364. Quoted in *The Observer*, August 28, 1949.
365. *The Goon Show*, with Peter Sellers, Spike Milligan, and others, ran on BBC radio from 1951 to 1958.
366. As given in H.
367. *The Comments of Moung Ka*.
368, 369. *The Catcher in the Rye*, 1951.
370. *Nausea*, January 1932.
372. *New York Times Magazine*, 1953.
374. *Best Sports Stories*, 1978.
378. "A Guide to Some of the Lesser Ballets," in *Without Feathers*, 1975.
379. As given in I.
381. In concert at the Hungry i in San Francisco, July 1965.
384. Ascribes to Katharine Hepburn in N.
387. As given in R.
388. *Who's Nobody in America*, by Fulwiler and Evans, 1981.
390. Reported by Herb Caen in *The San Francisco Chronicle*, April 24, 1980.
392. As given in N.
395. In various newspapers, 1978.
396. Quoted in Terence O'Flaherty's column, *The San Francisco Chronicle*, March 18, 1980.
397. Rewritten to conform to current postal rates.
404. Also said of other people.
405. *Newsweek*, March 28, 1960.
406, 407. See 263.
412. *Duck Soup*, 1933.
416. As given in N.
418. See 34.
424. *The Case of Wagner*.
425. *A View From a Broad*, 1980.
427. As given in N.
428. *Chips Off the Old Benchley*, 1949.
432. *The Constant Wife*, 1926.
433. *Our Betters*, 1923.
434. See 113.
435. *Inside Mr. Enderby*, 1968.
436. *Farewell, My Lovely*, 1940.

437. 1962.
440. In an interview with Barbara Walters.
441. JC was a writer for the *New York Post*.
443. *Unreliable Memoirs*, 1981.
444. The author probably is Paul Valéry (1871–1945) and not Arthur C. Clarke.
446. BH to RB.
447. As given in Q.
450. As recalled by Andre Previn and quoted by Herb Caen, *The San Francisco Chronicle*, February 1982.
451. The line "Forgive your enemies, but do not forget them," appears in the 1927 silent movie *Napoleon*, written and directed by Abel Gance.
453. *Finishing Touches*, Act III, 1973.
454. *Soon To Be a Major Motion Picture*, 1980.
456. As given in E.
457. Quoted in *A Thinking Man's Guide to Baseball*, 1967, by Leonard Koppet.
464. Quoted by Anatole Broyard in *The New York Times Book Review*, June 7, 1981.
465. *The Cat and the King*, 1981.
466. From an article on parental advice by Anthony Brown, distributed by *The Los Angeles Times* Syndicate.
467. *Rowing Toward Eden*, 1981.
469. As quoted by *The PG&E Progress*, January 1981.
474. Quoted by Dave Kindred in *The Washington Post*.
477. RL to RB.
478. In his syndicated newspaper column.
483. In an article on the death of *Scanlon's Magazine*, *Harper's*, April 1981.
485. In a letter to Sir Frederick Pollock.
488. In the story "Tlon, Uqbar, Orbis Tertius."
489. *The Young Immigrants*, 1920.
493. *The Medusa and the Snail*. 1979.
497. *Consenting Adults*, 1981.
504. And not his countryman, Hermann Goering.
507. See 270.
508. See 270.
509. A slightly different version appears in Herb Caen's column in *The San Francisco Chronicle*, May 1978. Mr. Wegner can be found at Trinity University in San Antonio, Texas.

512. Quoted by Merla Zellerbach in *The San Francisco Chronicle*, December 31, 1980.
515. *Dialogues in Limbo*, 1925.
516. *The Winter's Tale*.
521. *New York Times Book Review*, May 8, 1979.
523, 524. MH was a professor of Greek and Latin at Columbia.
530. *How to Prosper in the Coming Bad Years*, 1979.
534. Quoted in *Funny People*, by Steve Allen, 1981.
536. *The San Francisco Chronicle*, February 9, 1981.
538. *Household Hints*, 1966.
541. As given in M.
542. *Write If You Get Work*, 1975.
543. As given in F.
544. From a letter dated 1796.
545. *The Fall*, 1957.
546. *The Flying Inn*, 1912.
548. In a letter to Charles Green Shaw.
549. Quoted by Aldous Huxley in *Heaven and Hell*, 1956.
550. *The San Francisco Chronicle*, January 21, 1982.
551. Quoted by Herb Caen, *The San Francisco Chronicle*, February 14, 1982.
552. By Erskine & Moran, 1981.
553. As given in N.
555. Quoted in *The Wall Street Journal*.
559. *The Model Millionaire*, 1887.
560. *The Love Nest*, 1963.
561. *The Mythmakers*, 1979.
569. *Faust*, 1808.
570. *The Last Word*.
571. *Why I Am Not a Christian*, 1950.
574. *The Capitalist Handbook*.
576. From her *Letters*.
577. *The History of the French Revolution*, 1837.
579. June 26, 1979.
580. See 488.
581. Compiled from various interviews.
583. As given in K.
585. See 583.
586. *The Tonight Show*, February 7, 1979.
588. See 180.
590. From a poem titled "Put Back Those Whiskers, I Know You," in *Good Intentions*, 1942.

591. *Many Long Years Ago*, 1945.
592. Quoted by George Bernard Shaw in the preface to *Androcles and the Lion*, 1912.
593. *The House of the Seven Gables*, 1851.
598. *My Ten Years in a Quandary*, 1936.
599. See 598.
600. Quoted by Leacock in *Humor: Its Theory and Technique*, 1935.
601. *Too Much College*, 1941.
602. "Gertrude the Governess," in *Nonsense Novels*, 1914.
605. As given in F.
606. As given in F.
607. "Selections From the Allen Notebooks," in *Without Feathers*, 1975.
609. *Versus*, 1949.
611. JH to RB about a television talk-show host, 1970.
612. As given in K.
613. See 140.
614. See 34.
615. *Polite Conversation*, 1738.
619. *New York Times Book Review*.
620. As given in B.
622. Before his retirement in 1981, KHA was in charge of the San Francisco Opera Company.
624. *Dialogues*, 1954.
626. As given in F.
628. To C. A. Dana, April 1865.
629. *Euphues*, 1579.
633. As quoted by Allison Silver in *The New York Times Book Review*, February 28, 1982.
636. As given in K.

Principal Sources of Artwork

❧✿❧

Harter's Picture Archives for Collage and Illustration, edited by Jim Harter and containing over 300 nineteenth-century cuts.
Music, A Pictorial Archive of Woodcuts & Engravings, selected by Jim Harter and containing 841 illustrations.
Men, A Pictorial Archive from Nineteenth-Century Sources, selected by Jim Harter and containing 412 illustrations.
Women, A Pictorial Archive from Nineteenth-Century Sources, selected by Jim Harter and containing 391 illustrations.
Picture Sourcebook for Collage and Decoupage, edited by Edmund V. Gillon, Jr., and containing over 300 illustrations.

The above five titles are published by Dover Publications.

Index of Authors

Index of Subjects and Key Words

About the Author

Robert Byrne has been a cab driver, pool hustler, college humor magazine editor, highway design engineer, trade journal editor, and novelist. THE 637 BEST THINGS ANYBODY EVER SAID is an outgrowth of a notebook he has been keeping for years. Why has he selected "637" quotations instead of, say 630 or 650? "I didn't want to leave any good ones out," he says, "and I didn't want to pad it." Robert Byrne lives in San Rafael, California, where he is at work on a new novel.